MY FIRST ACTIVITY BOOK

DRAW + LEARN

PLACES

D1515254

by Harriet Ziefert

BLUE APPLE

Art by Tanya Roitman

Text copyright © 2012 by Harriet Ziefert
Illustrations copyright © 2012 by Tanya Roitman
All rights reserved
Published in the United States 2012 by
Blue Apple Books, 515 Valley Street, Maplewood, NJ 07040
www.blueapplebooks.com
04/12   Printed in Shenzhen, China
ISBN: 978-1-60905-217-1

2 4 6 8 10 9 7 5 3

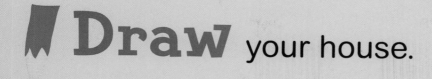

Draw your house.

Name _____ Date _____

A house is made of many shapes.

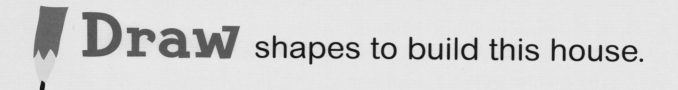 **Draw** shapes to build this house.

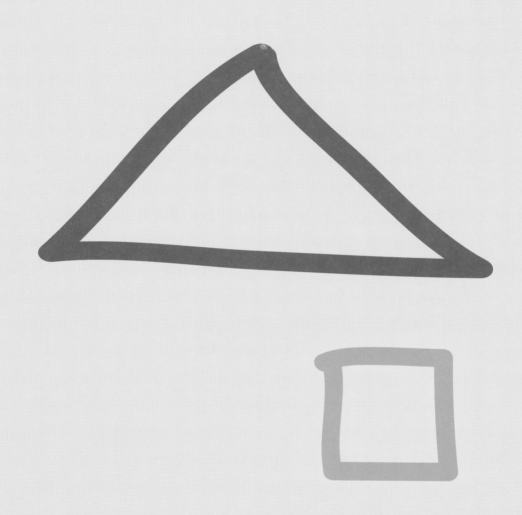

Draw This house has a roof, a door, and a window. Give it a chimney and bushes. Does it need flowers?

 **Color** this house.

 **Draw** lines to finish the house.

 Color

 **Color** who lives in this house.

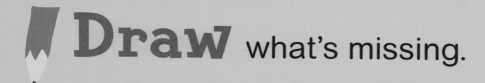 **Draw** what's missing.

Color

 # Color this house.

Draw

Some houses are small.

 **Draw** a small house.

Here are more small houses.
Finish coloring the houses and the kids.

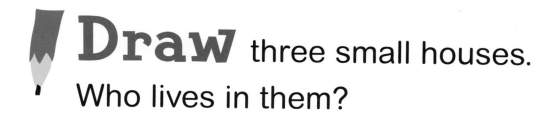 **Draw** three small houses. Who lives in them?

SMALL

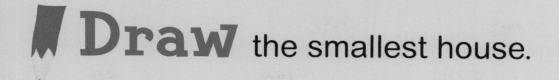 **Draw** the smallest house.

SMALLER   SMALLEST

Some houses have gardens.

Some houses have yards.

 **Draw**

 Color

 **Draw** your house.

Here's a kitchen.

 **Draw** your kitchen.

Here's a bathroom.

Draw your bathroom.

Here's a bedroom.

 **Draw** your bedroom.

 # Draw your street.

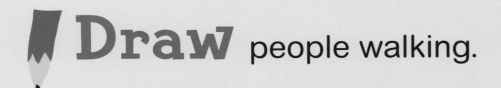 **Draw** people walking.

Color

Color

Here's a lemonade stand. Make a sign.

Draw and Color

Here's a tree house.

Draw

A garage is a house for a car.

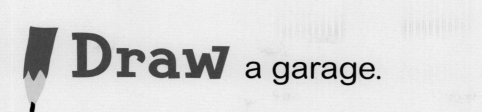

Draw a garage.

This is a firehouse.
 **Draw** a firefighter.

 **Draw** a firehouse.

Some dogs have houses.

 **Draw** another doghouse.

Draw a little house for a little mouse.

 **Draw** a big house for a big elephant.

A rabbit house is called a hutch.
Color the rabbits. Add whiskers.

 **Draw** a hutch.

Draw a birdhouse.

 # Color

A lighthouse is a house for a lightkeeper.

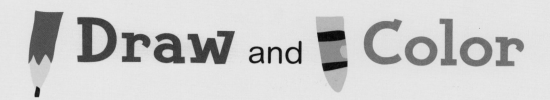 Draw and Color

A barn is a house for animals.

Draw and Color

A tent is a house for campers.

Draw and Color

A palace is a house for a princess.

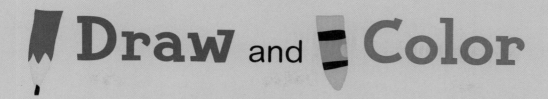

Draw and Color

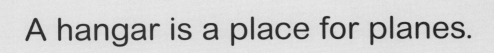

A hangar is a place for planes.

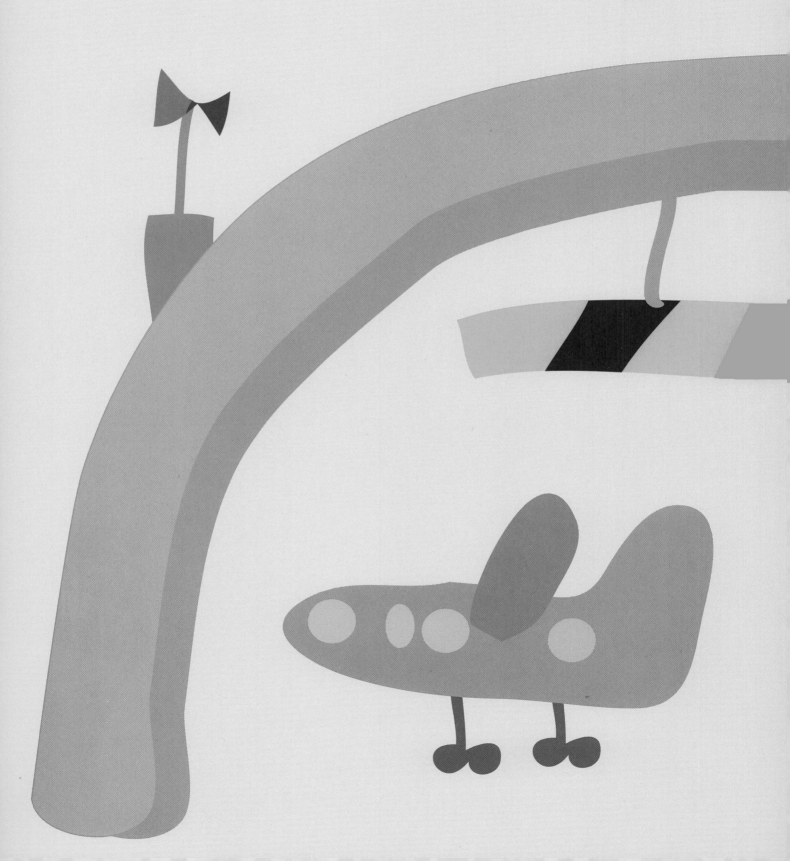

Draw another plane.

An igloo is a house for an Eskimo.

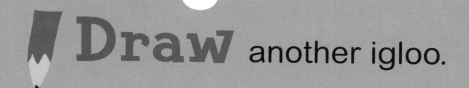 **Draw** another igloo.

Color

Draw

Color

✏️ Draw

Color

FLOWERS

 # Draw

This is a toy store. What can
you see in the windows?

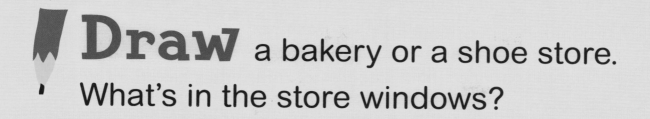 **Draw** a bakery or a shoe store. What's in the store windows?

An apartment house is a
house for many families.

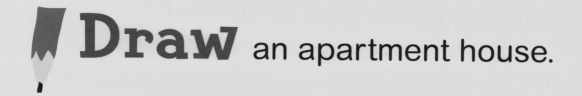

Draw an apartment house.

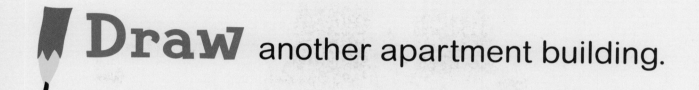 **Draw** another apartment building.

Draw

 # Color

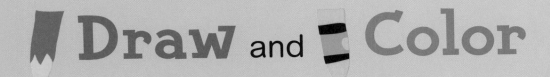

Draw and Color

TALLER

TALL

TALLEST

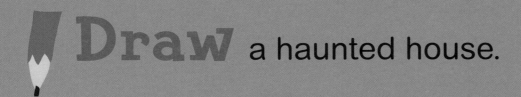 **Draw** a haunted house.

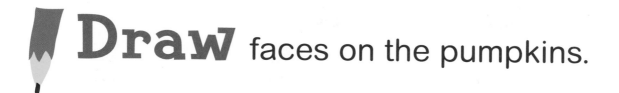 **Draw** faces on the pumpkins.

Draw the fireworks and the people watching.

Color the windows.

Here's a park at night.
Color the trees and the flowers.